GRAPHIC EXPEDITIONS

CAPTURED BY PIRATES!

AN *Isabel Soto* HISTORY ADVENTURE

by Agnieszka Biskup
illustrated by Roger Stewart

Consultant:
Cindy Stavely
Executive Director
St. Augustine Pirate and Treasure Museum
St. Augustine, Florida

CAPSTONE PRESS
a capstone imprint

Graphic Library is published by Capstone Press,
1710 Roe Crest Drive, North Mankato, Minnesota 56003.
www.capstonepub.com

Printed in the United States of America in Stevens Point, Wisconsin.
102011
006404WZS12

Books published by Capstone Press are manufactured with paper containing at least 10 percent post-consumer waste.

Library of Congress Cataloging-in-Publication Data
Biskup, Agnieszka.
Captured by pirates! : an Isabel Soto history adventure / by Agnieszka Biskup ; illustrated by Roger Stewart.
p. cm.—(Graphic library. Graphic expeditions)
Includes bibliographical references and index.
Summary: "In graphic novel format, follows the adventures of Isabel Soto as she learns about pirate life during the Golden Age of Piracy"—Provided by publisher.
ISBN 978-1-4296-7545-1 (library binding)
ISBN 978-1-4296-7991-6 (paperback)
1. Pirates—Juvenile literature. 2. Hijacking of ships—Juvenile literature. I. Stewart, Roger, ill. II. Title. III. Series
G535.B5 2012
910.4'5—dc23 2011028642

Designer
Alison Thiele

Editor
Aaron Sautter

Production Specialist
Laura Manthe

Photo credits: Shutterstock/Jim Parkin, 11 inset, Philip Lange, 19 inset

Design elements: Shutterstock/Chen Ping Hung (framed edge design); mmmm (world map design); Mushakesa (abstract lines design); Najin (old parchment design)

TABLE OF CONTENTS

OUT TO SEA ---------------------------- 4

CAPTURED! -------------------------- 6

LIVING BY THE CODE ---------------- 12

A PIRATE'S "MERCY" ------------- 20

SEEKING HYDE -------------------- 24

MORE ABOUT PIRATES AND ISABEL SOTO 28–29

GLOSSARY 30

READ MORE 31

INTERNET SITES 31

INDEX 32

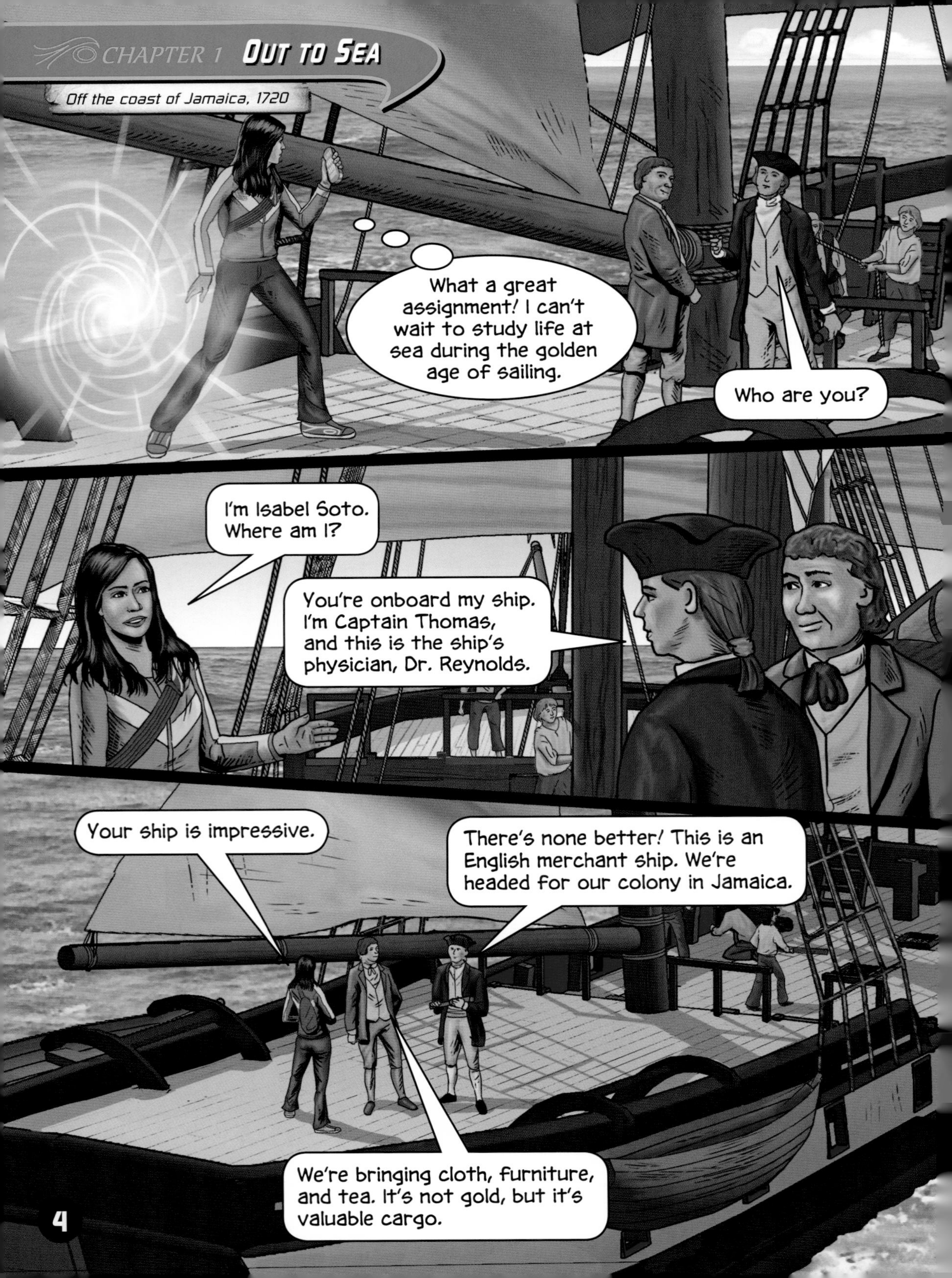
CHAPTER 1 OUT TO SEA
Off the coast of Jamaica, 1720
What a great assignment! I can't wait to study life at sea during the golden age of sailing.
Who are you?
I'm Isabel Soto. Where am I?
You're onboard my ship. I'm Captain Thomas, and this is the ship's physician, Dr. Reynolds.
Your ship is impressive.
There's none better! This is an English merchant ship. We're headed for our colony in Jamaica.
We're bringing cloth, furniture, and tea. It's not gold, but it's valuable cargo.

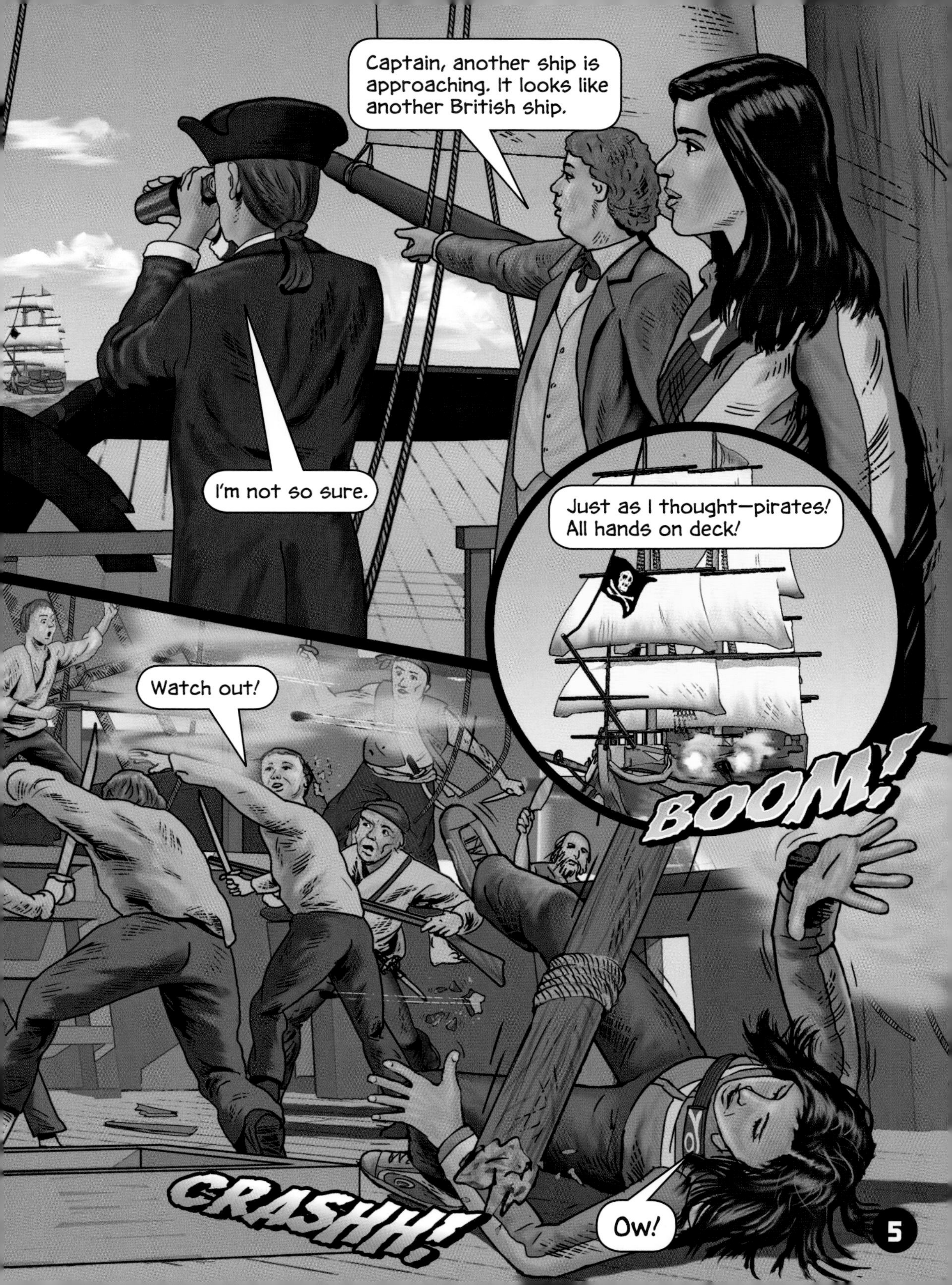

Captain, another ship is approaching. It looks like another British ship.
I'm not so sure.
Just as I thought—pirates! All hands on deck!
BOOM!
Watch out!
CRASHH!
Ow!

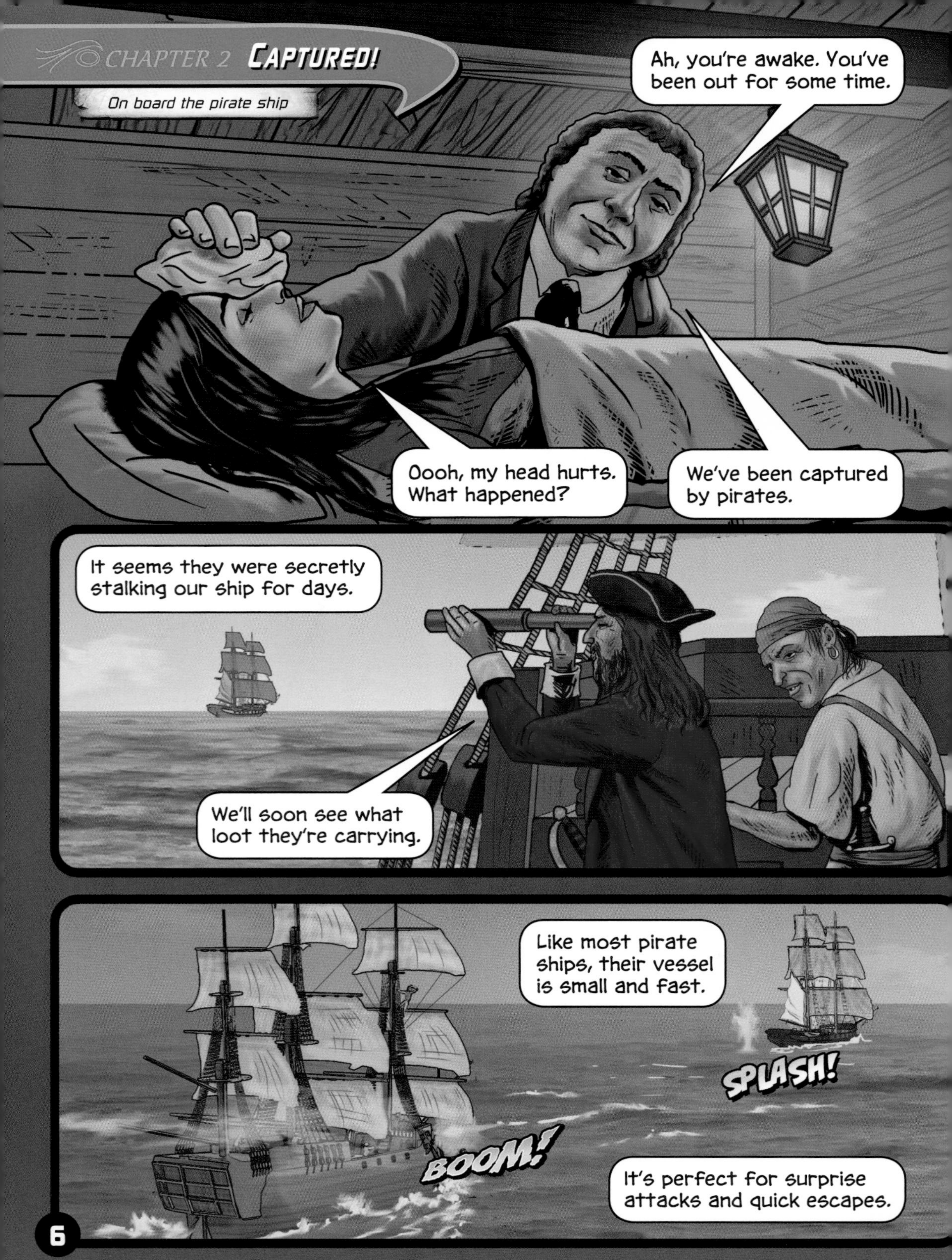
CHAPTER 2 CAPTURED!
On board the pirate ship
Ah, you're awake. You've been out for some time.
Oooh, my head hurts. What happened?
We've been captured by pirates.
It seems they were secretly stalking our ship for days.
We'll soon see what loot they're carrying.
Like most pirate ships, their vessel is small and fast.
SPLASH!
BOOM!
It's perfect for surprise attacks and quick escapes.

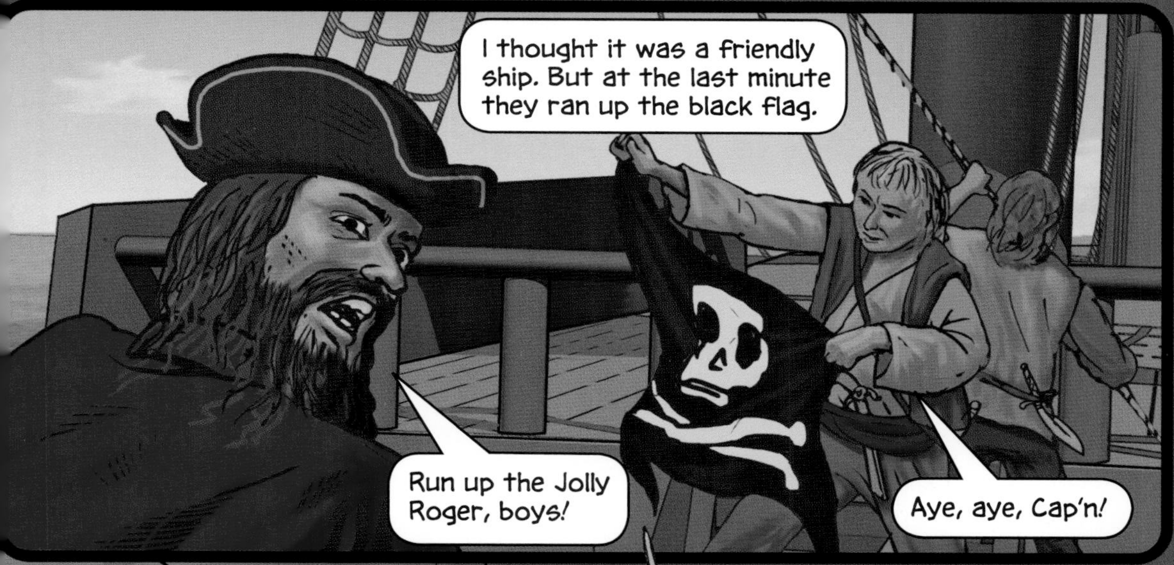
I thought it was a friendly ship. But at the last minute they ran up the black flag.
Run up the Jolly Roger, boys!
Aye, aye, Cap'n!

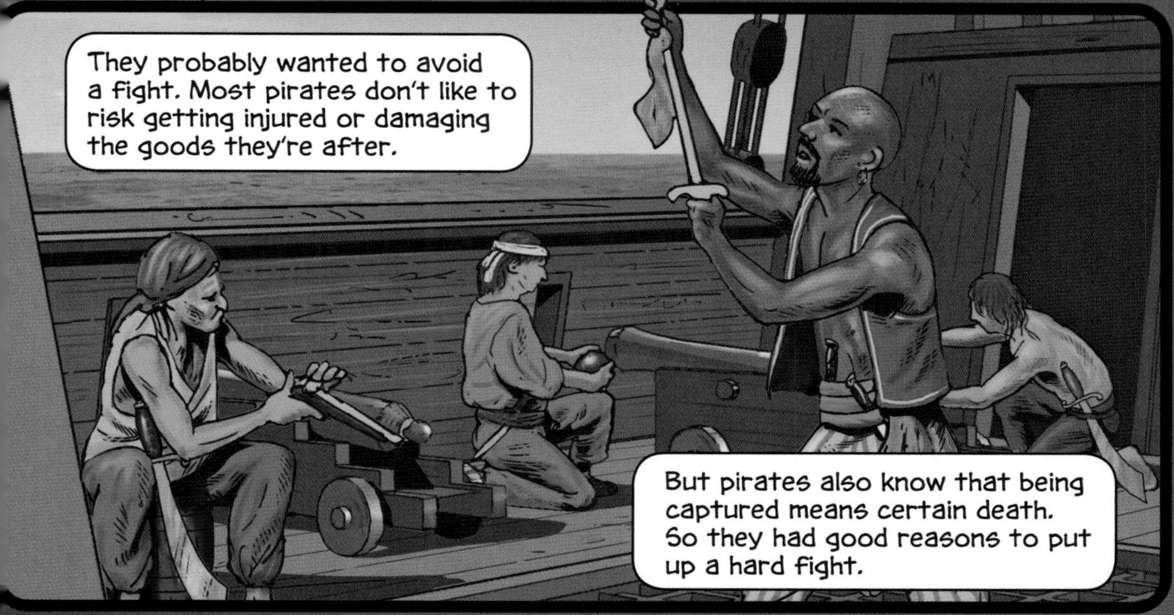
They probably wanted to avoid a fight. Most pirates don't like to risk getting injured or damaging the goods they're after.
But pirates also know that being captured means certain death. So they had good reasons to put up a hard fight.

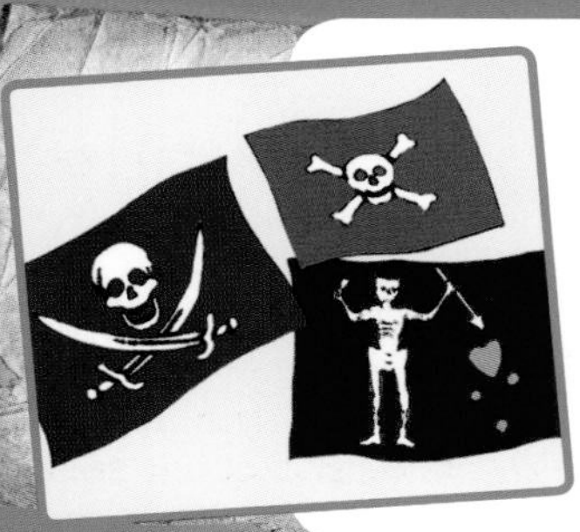

THE JOLLY ROGER

Pirate flags were not always black with a white skull and crossbones. The name Jolly Roger comes from the French words *jolie rouge*, which means "pretty red." In the early days of piracy, pirates often flew red flags. Most pirates had their own designs that included symbols of death. The flag designs included skulls, skeletons, swords, bleeding hearts, and more.

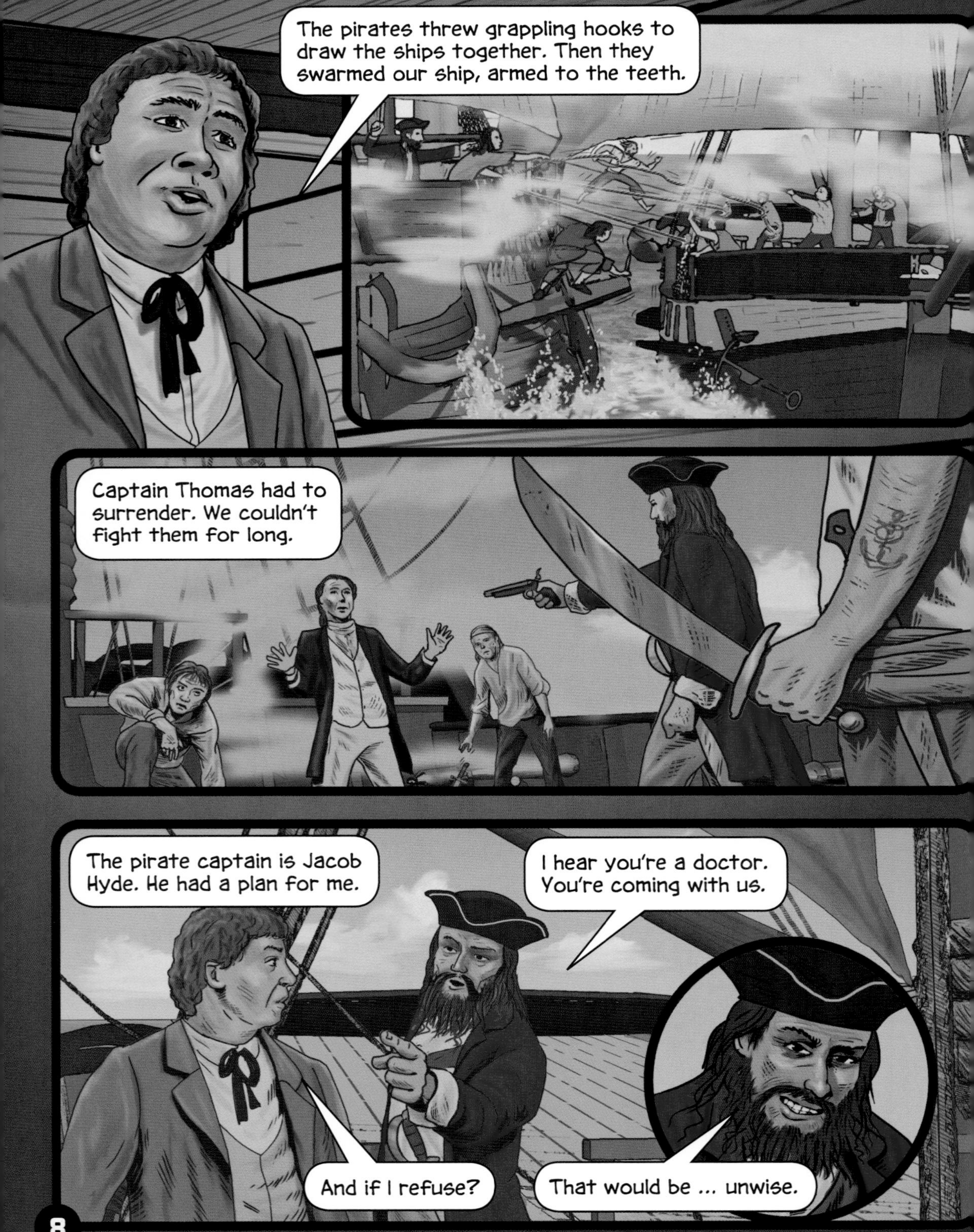
The pirates threw grappling hooks to draw the ships together. Then they swarmed our ship, armed to the teeth.
Captain Thomas had to surrender. We couldn't fight them for long.
The pirate captain is Jacob Hyde. He had a plan for me.
I hear you're a doctor. You're coming with us.
And if I refuse?
That would be ... unwise.

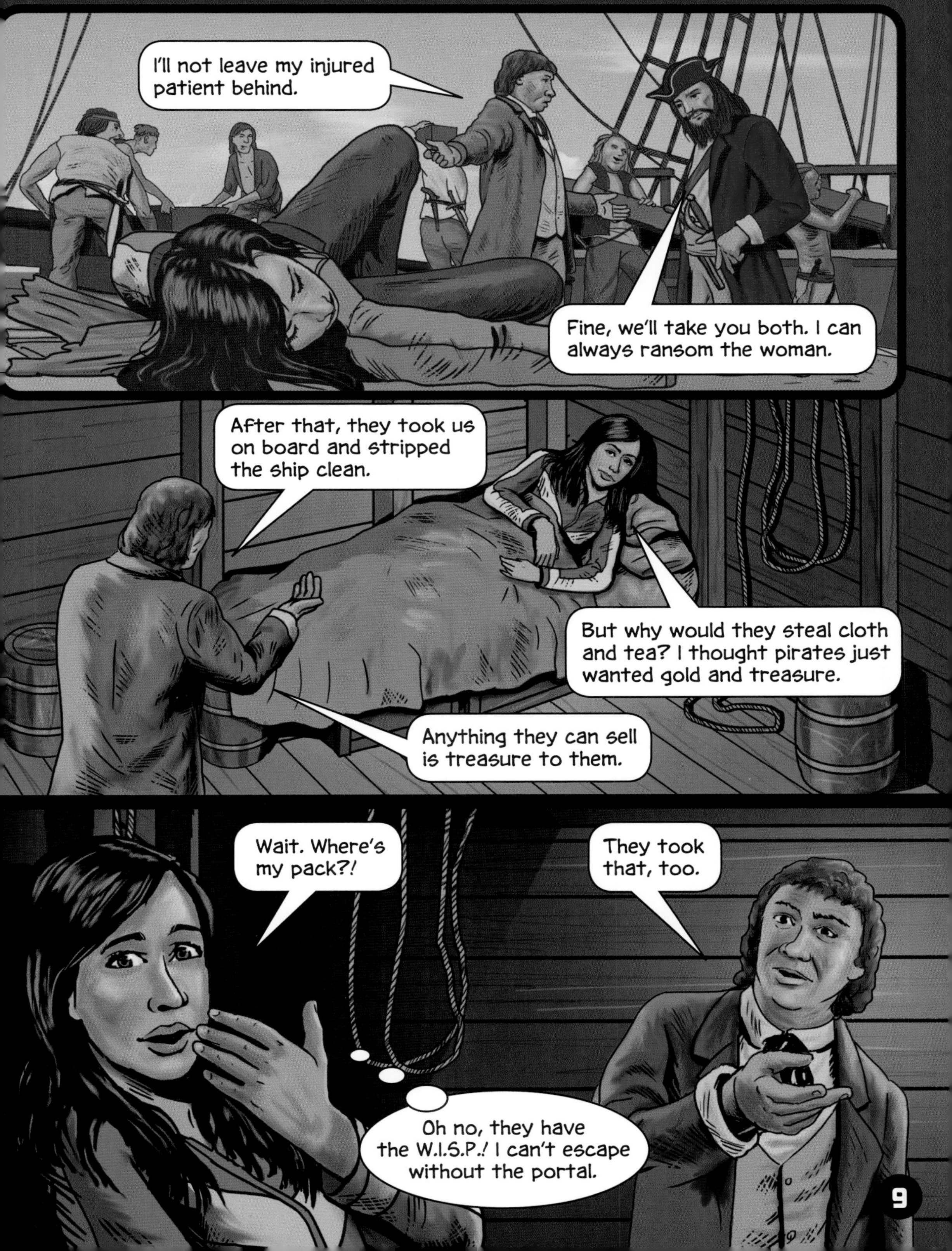
I'll not leave my injured patient behind.
Fine, we'll take you both. I can always ransom the woman.
After that, they took us on board and stripped the ship clean.
But why would they steal cloth and tea? I thought pirates just wanted gold and treasure.
Anything they can sell is treasure to them.
Wait. Where's my pack?!
They took that, too.
Oh no, they have the W.I.S.P.! I can't escape without the portal.

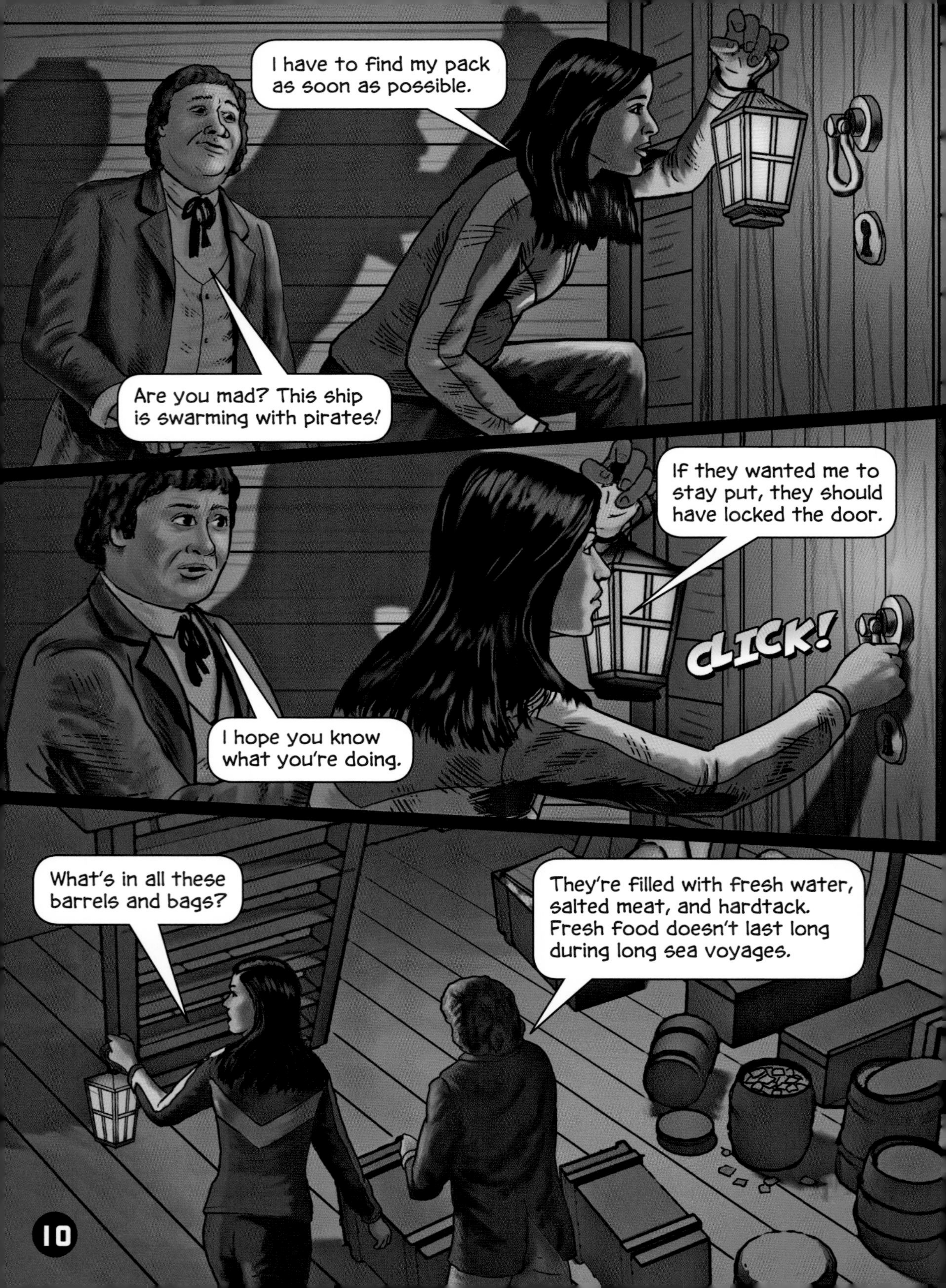
I have to find my pack as soon as possible.
Are you mad? This ship is swarming with pirates!
If they wanted me to stay put, they should have locked the door.
CLICK!
I hope you know what you're doing.
What's in all these barrels and bags?
They're filled with fresh water, salted meat, and hardtack. Fresh food doesn't last long during long sea voyages.

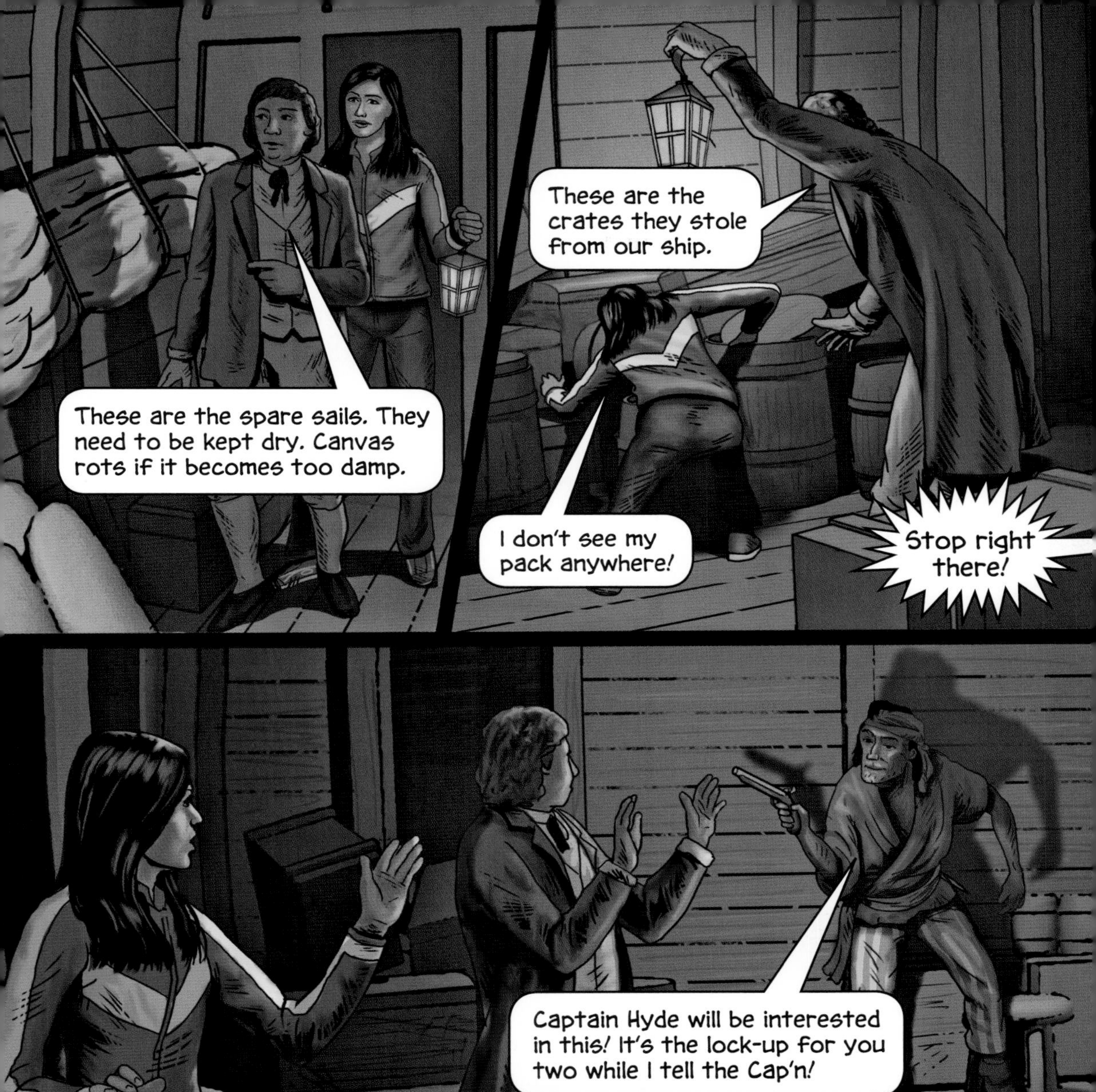

These are the spare sails. They need to be kept dry. Canvas rots if it becomes too damp.
These are the crates they stole from our ship.
I don't see my pack anywhere!
Stop right there!
Captain Hyde will be interested in this! It's the lock-up for you two while I tell the Cap'n!

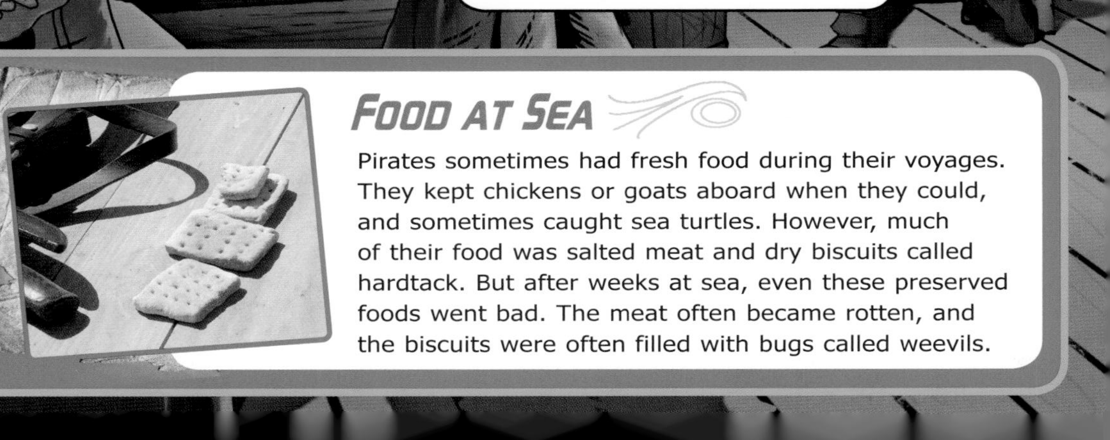

Food at Sea

Pirates sometimes had fresh food during their voyages. They kept chickens or goats aboard when they could, and sometimes caught sea turtles. However, much of their food was salted meat and dry biscuits called hardtack. But after weeks at sea, even these preserved foods went bad. The meat often became rotten, and the biscuits were often filled with bugs called weevils.

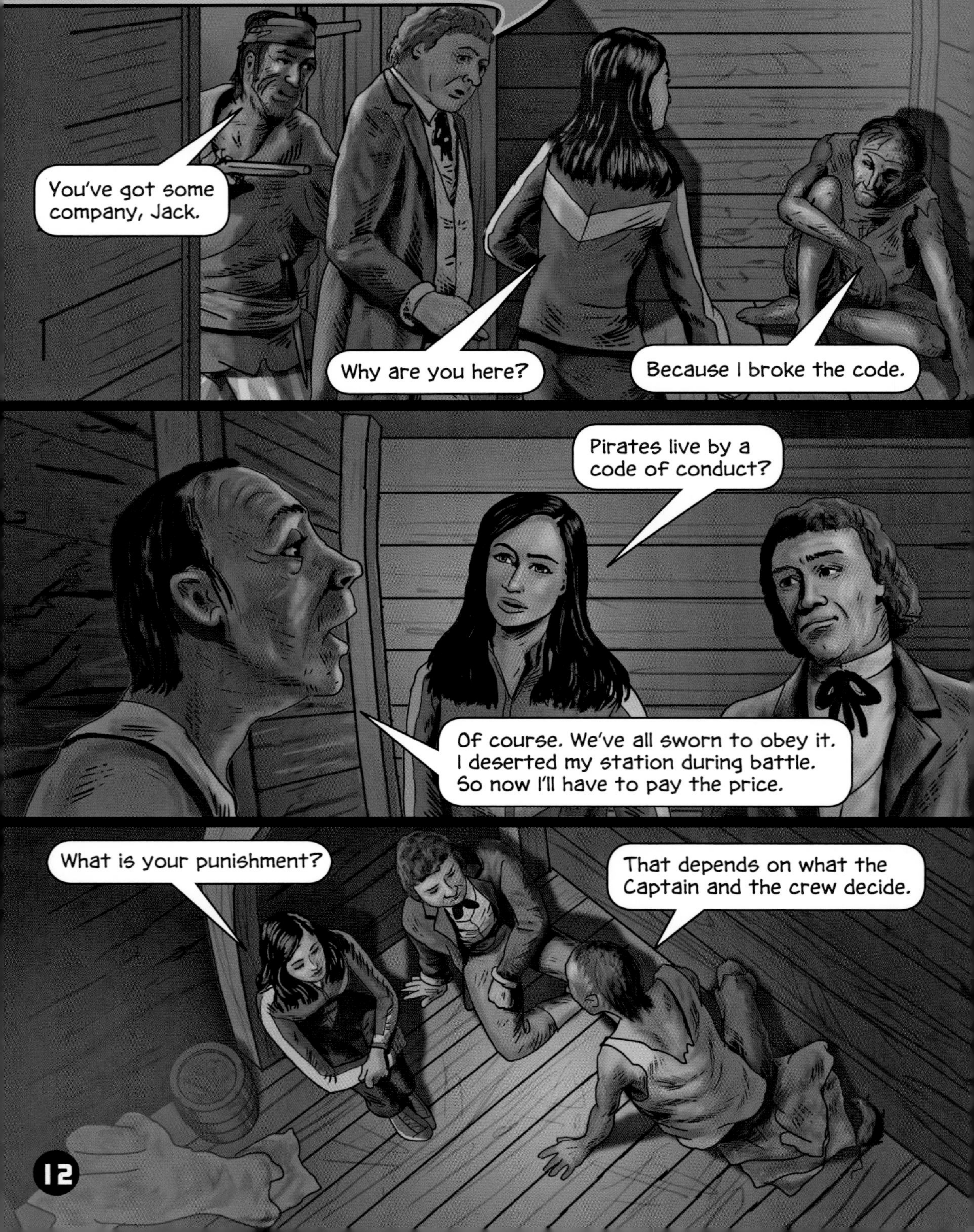
You've got some company, Jack.
Why are you here?
Because I broke the code.
Pirates live by a code of conduct?
Of course. We've all sworn to obey it. I deserted my station during battle. So now I'll have to pay the price.
What is your punishment?
That depends on what the Captain and the crew decide.

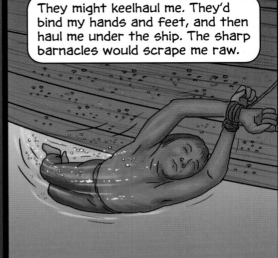

I could be flogged, or whipped, with a cat-o'-nine-tails in front of the entire crew.

They might keelhaul me. They'd bind my hands and feet, and then haul me under the ship. The sharp barnacles would scrape me raw.

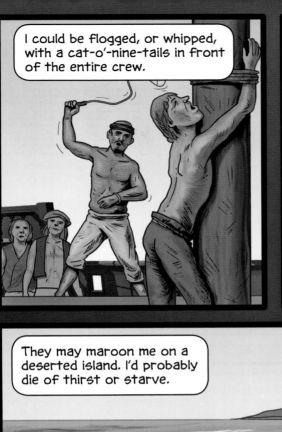

They may maroon me on a deserted island. I'd probably die of thirst or starve.

Or maybe they'll just kill me right away.

Will they make you walk the plank?

I've never heard of pirates doing that. I reckon they'd just toss me overboard to drown.

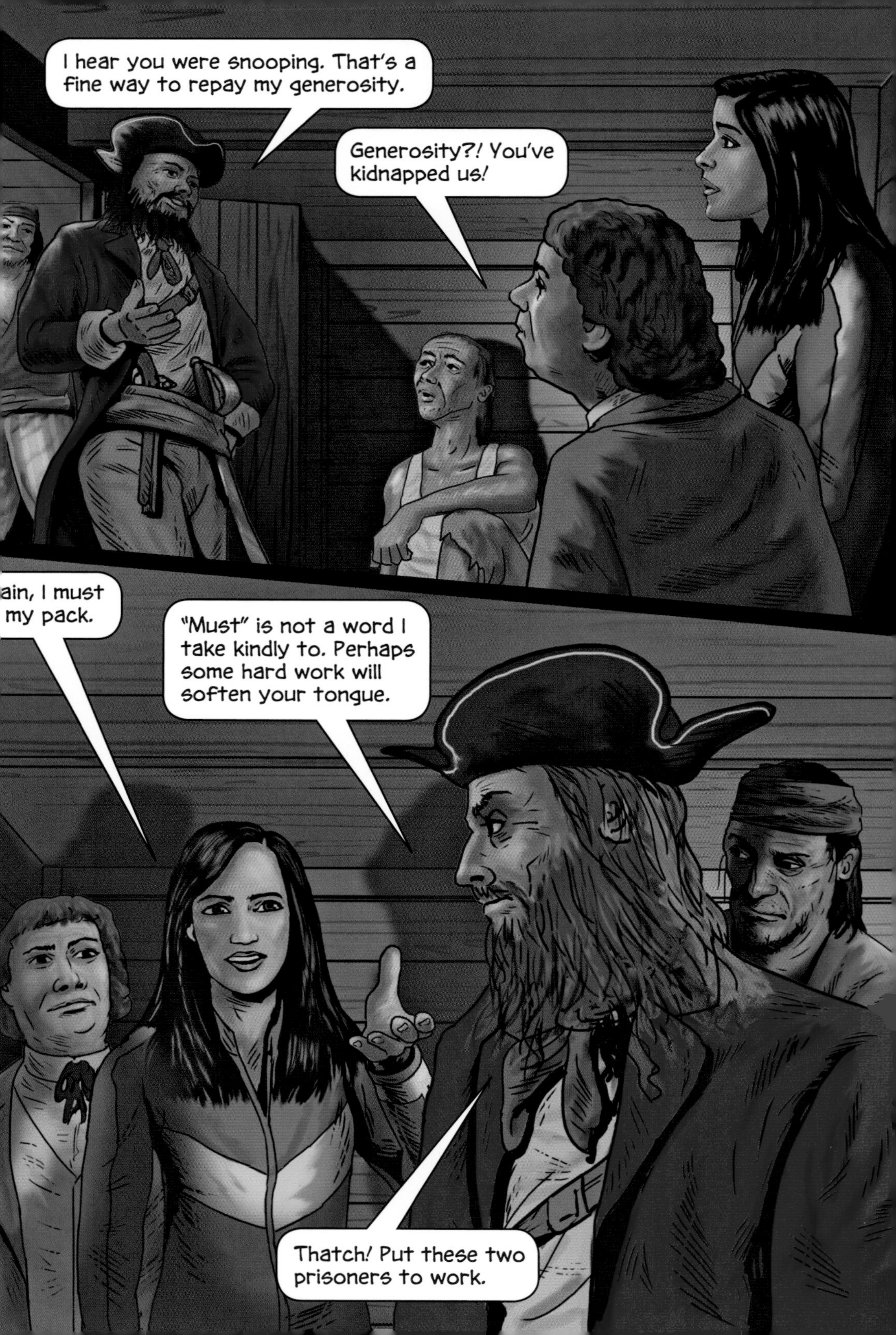
I hear you were snooping. That's a fine way to repay my generosity.
Generosity?! You've kidnapped us!
ain, I must my pack.
"Must" is not a word I take kindly to. Perhaps some hard work will soften your tongue.
Thatch! Put these two prisoners to work.

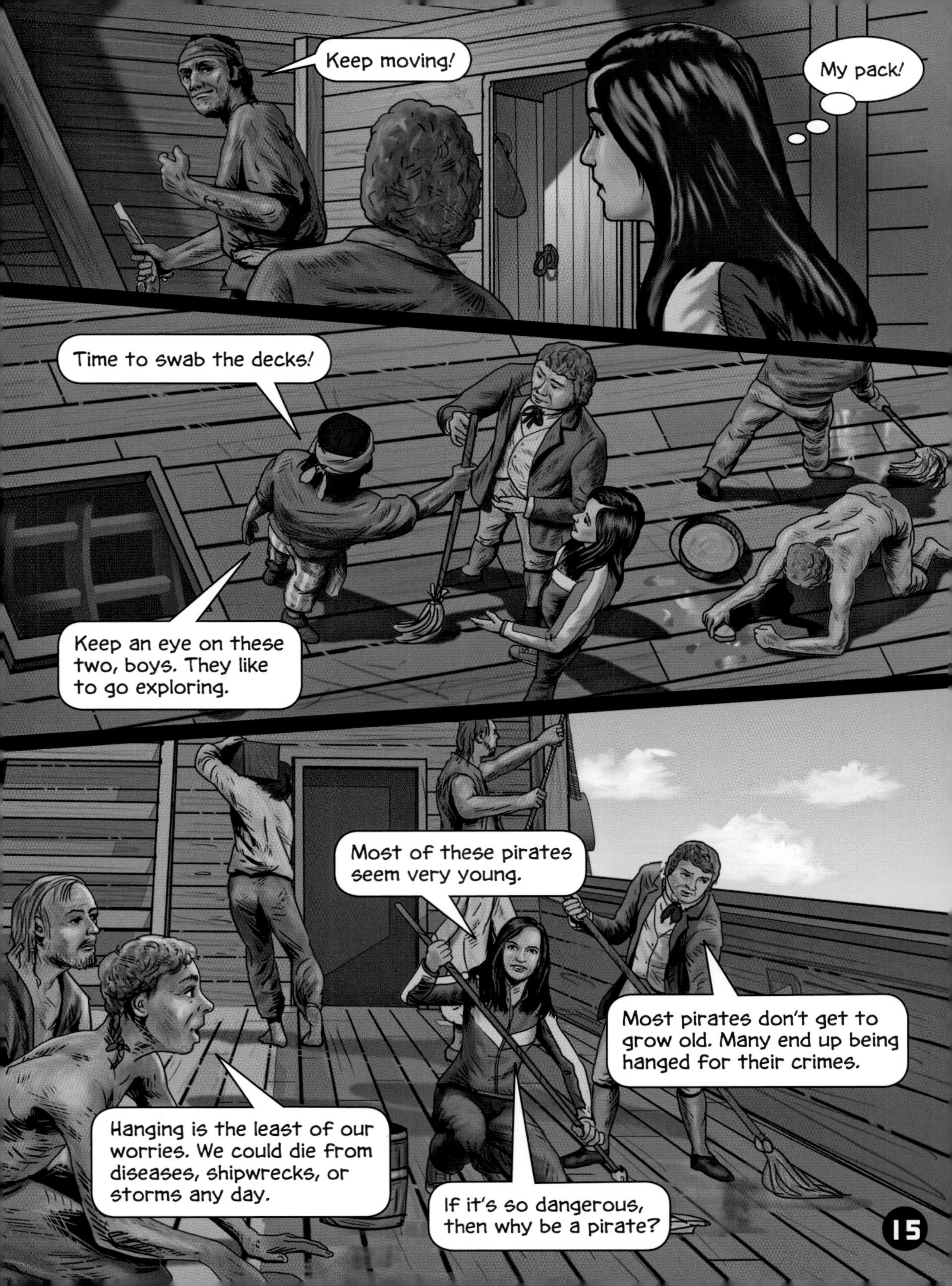

Keep moving!
My pack!
Time to swab the decks!
Keep an eye on these two, boys. They like to go exploring.
Most of these pirates seem very young.
Most pirates don't get to grow old. Many end up being hanged for their crimes.
Hanging is the least of our worries. We could die from diseases, shipwrecks, or storms any day.
If it's so dangerous, then why be a pirate?

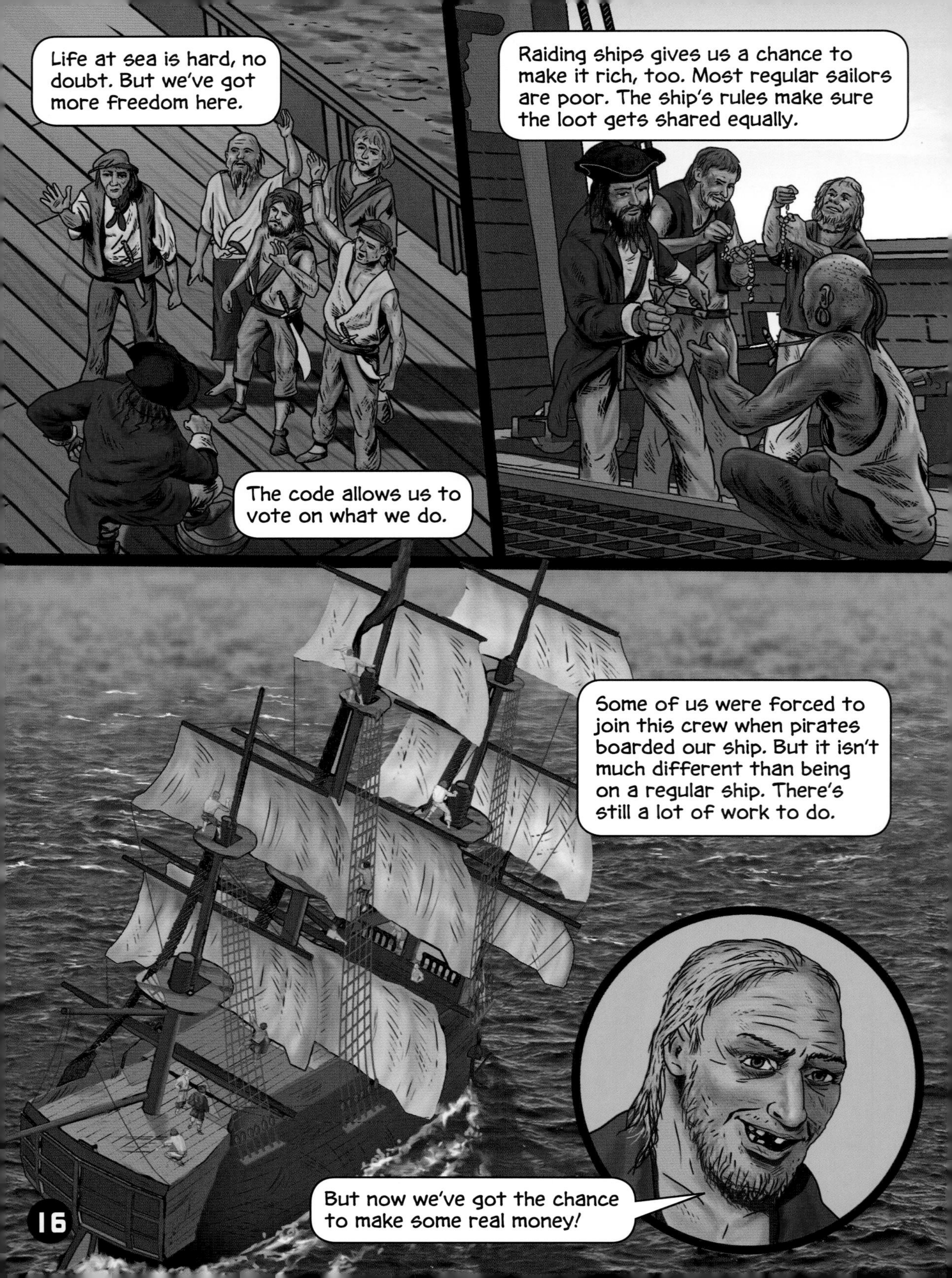

Life at sea is hard, no doubt. But we've got more freedom here.
The code allows us to vote on what we do.
Raiding ships gives us a chance to make it rich, too. Most regular sailors are poor. The ship's rules make sure the loot gets shared equally.
Some of us were forced to join this crew when pirates boarded our ship. But it isn't much different than being on a regular ship. There's still a lot of work to do.
But now we've got the chance to make some real money!

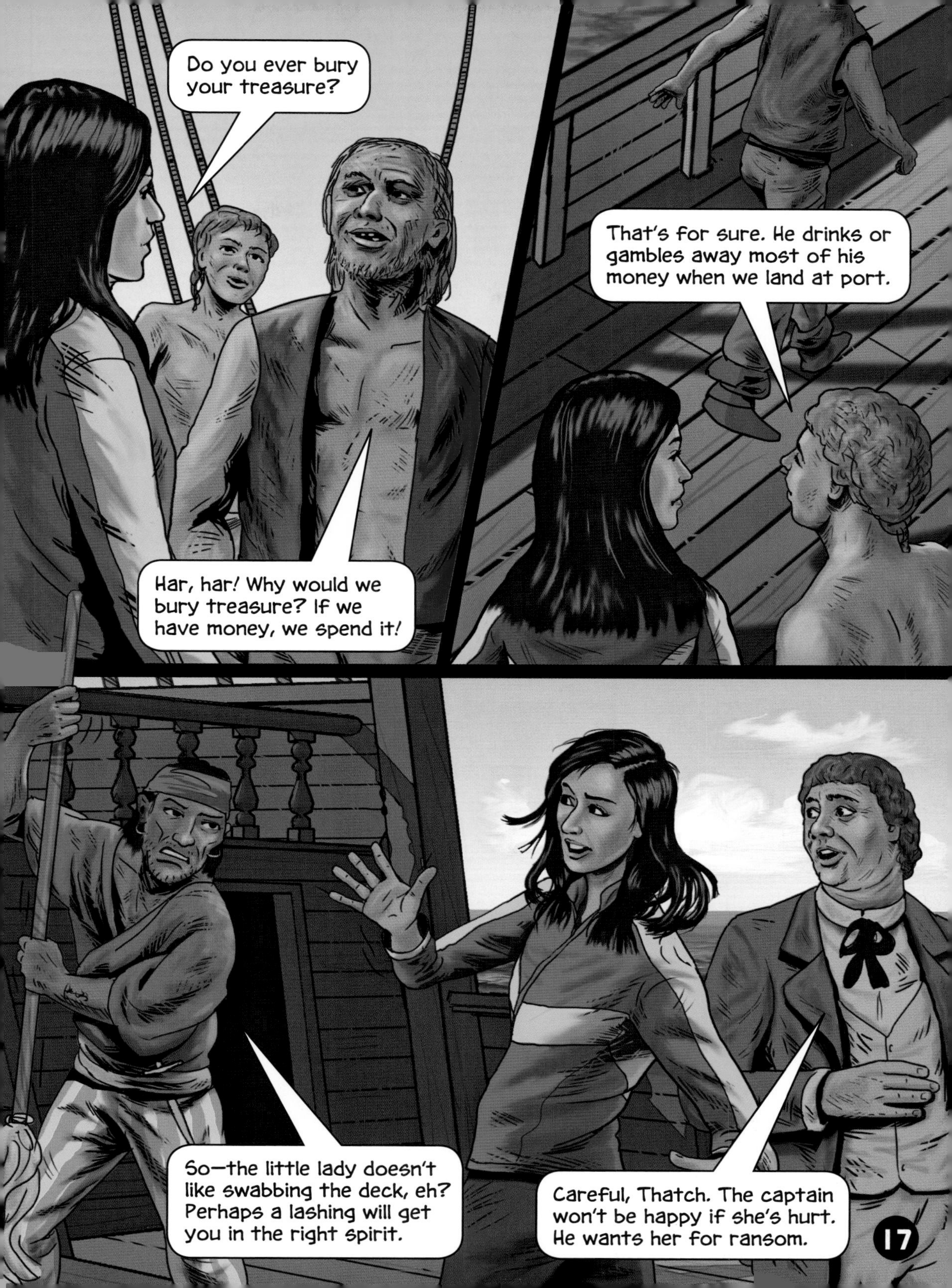
Do you ever bury your treasure?
Har, har! Why would we bury treasure? If we have money, we spend it!
That's for sure. He drinks or gambles away most of his money when we land at port.
So—the little lady doesn't like swabbing the deck, eh? Perhaps a lashing will get you in the right spirit.
Careful, Thatch. The captain won't be happy if she's hurt. He wants her for ransom.

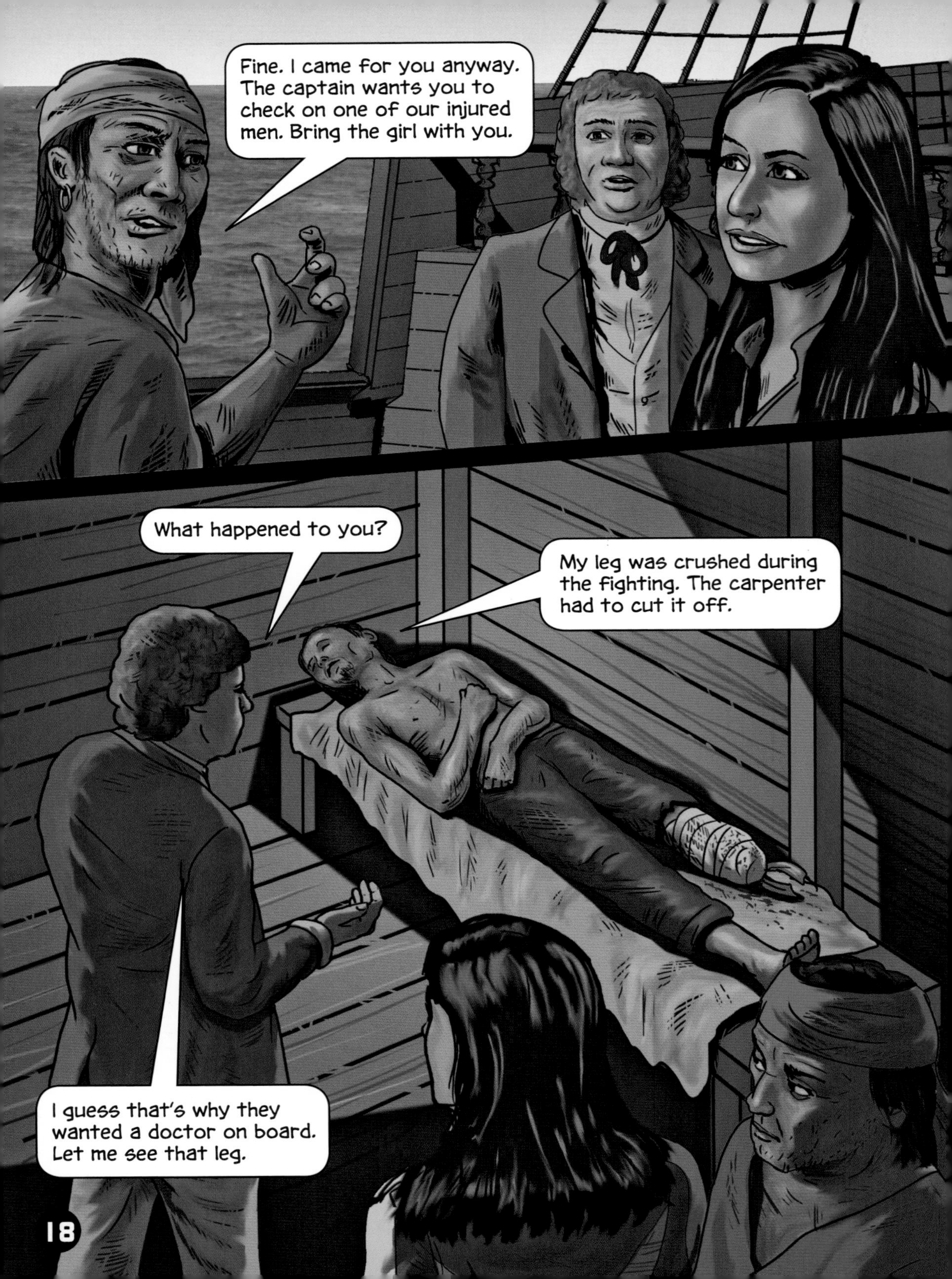
Fine. I came for you anyway. The captain wants you to check on one of our injured men. Bring the girl with you.
What happened to you?
My leg was crushed during the fighting. The carpenter had to cut it off.
I guess that's why they wanted a doctor on board. Let me see that leg.

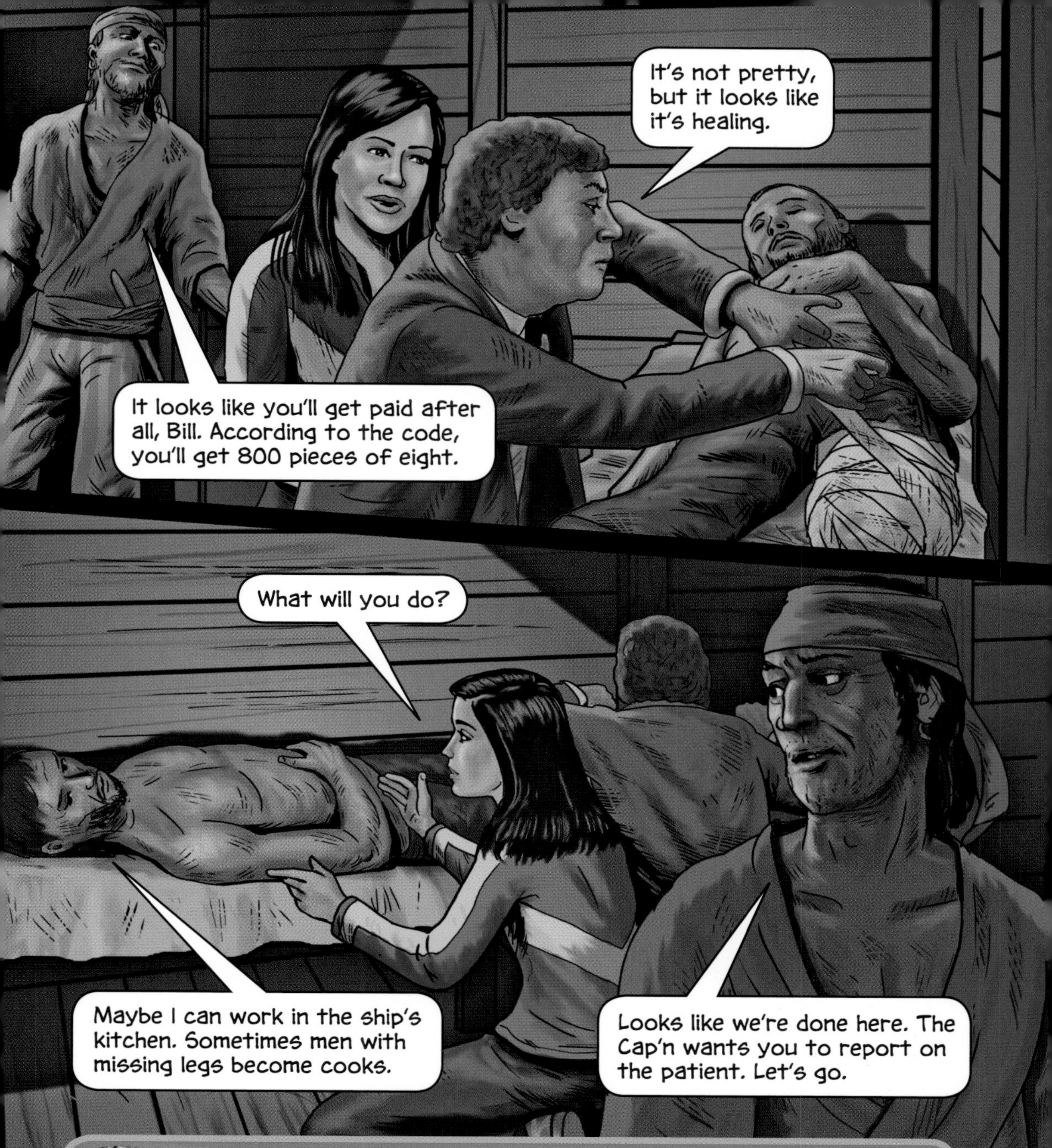
It's not pretty, but it looks like it's healing.
It looks like you'll get paid after all, Bill. According to the code, you'll get 800 pieces of eight.
What will you do?
Maybe I can work in the ship's kitchen. Sometimes men with missing legs become cooks.
Looks like we're done here. The Cap'n wants you to report on the patient. Let's go.

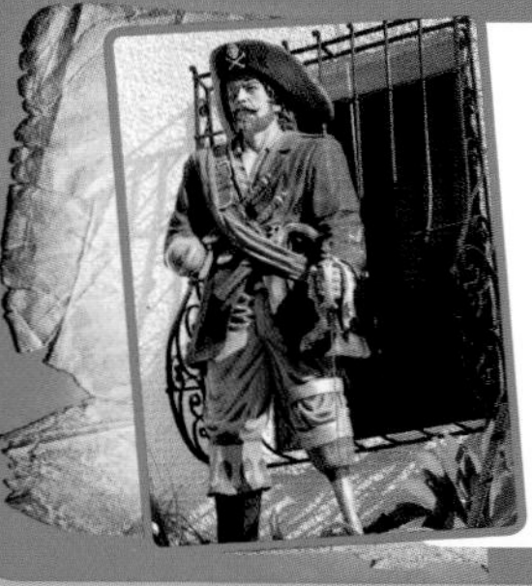

TREATING INJURIES

In the 1700s, the only way to treat badly injured arms and legs was to cut them off. A patient was usually held down while the injured limb was sawed off. Brandy or rum was used to control pain, but had little effect. When no doctor was available, the ship's carpenter performed the surgery. Many patients later died from infections.

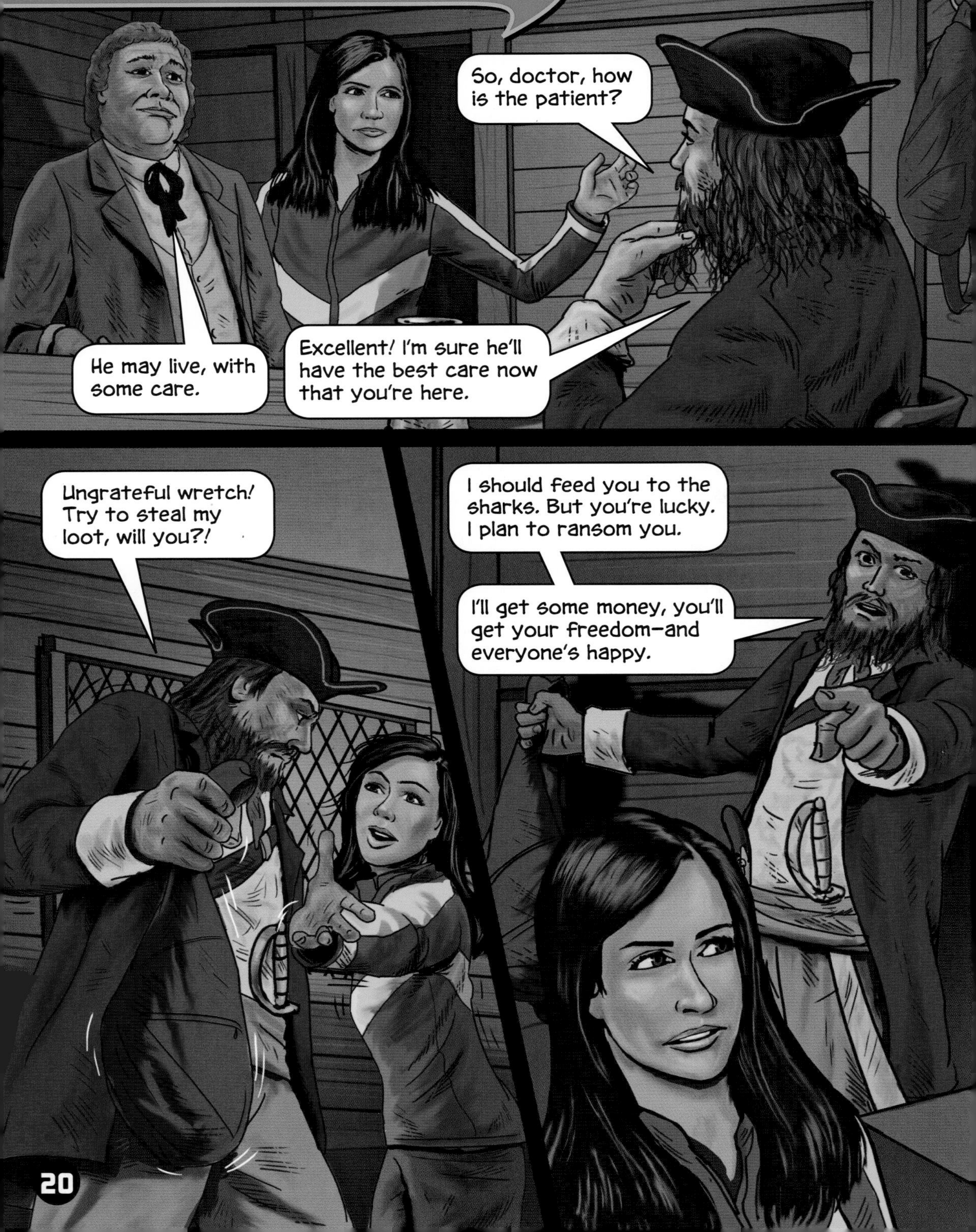
So, doctor, how is the patient?
He may live, with some care.
Excellent! I'm sure he'll have the best care now that you're here.
Ungrateful wretch! Try to steal my loot, will you?!
I should feed you to the sharks. But you're lucky. I plan to ransom you.
I'll get some money, you'll get your freedom—and everyone's happy.

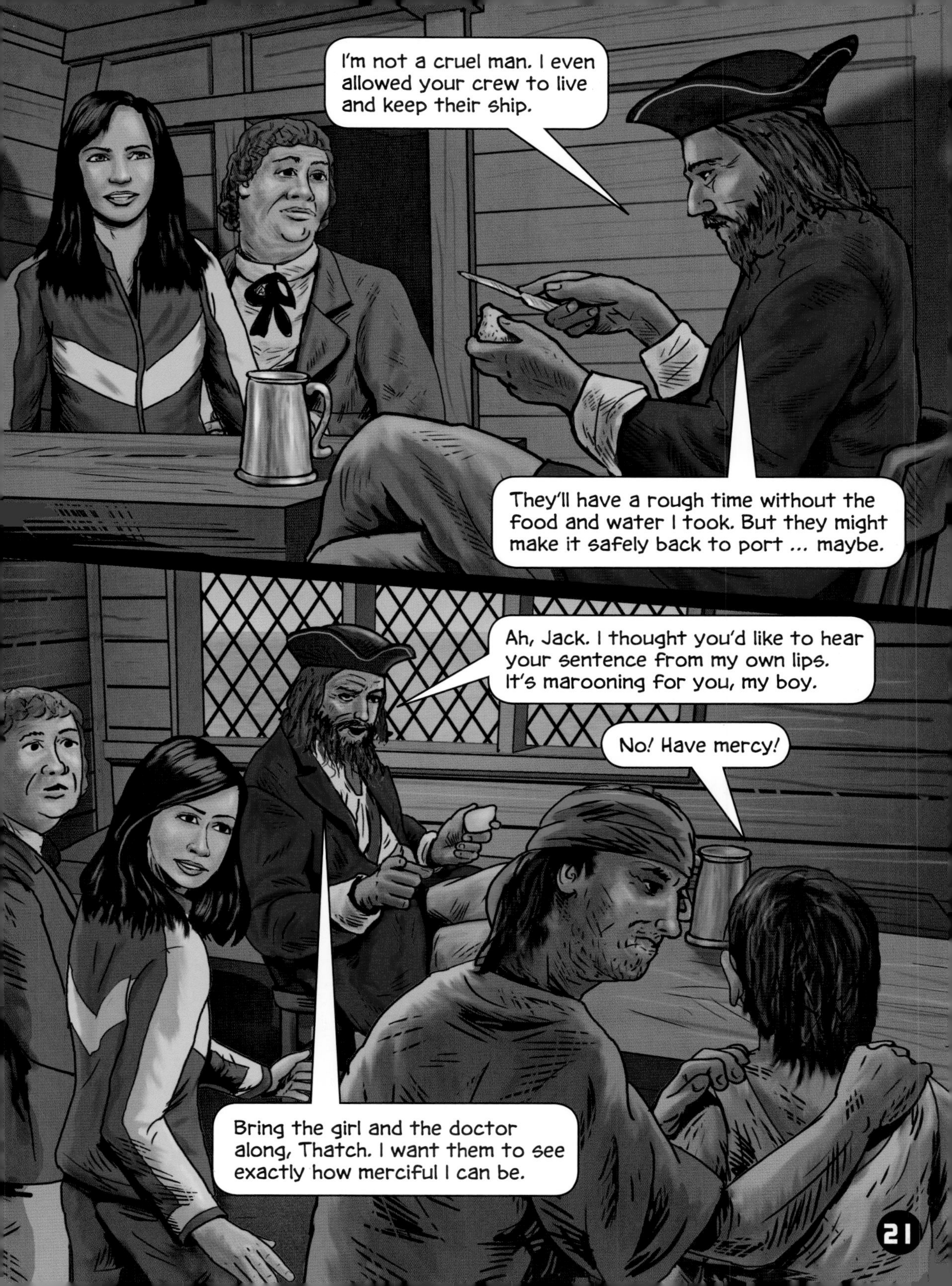
I'm not a cruel man. I even allowed your crew to live and keep their ship.
They'll have a rough time without the food and water I took. But they might make it safely back to port ... maybe.
Ah, Jack. I thought you'd like to hear your sentence from my own lips. It's marooning for you, my boy.
No! Have mercy!
Bring the girl and the doctor along, Thatch. I want them to see exactly how merciful I can be.

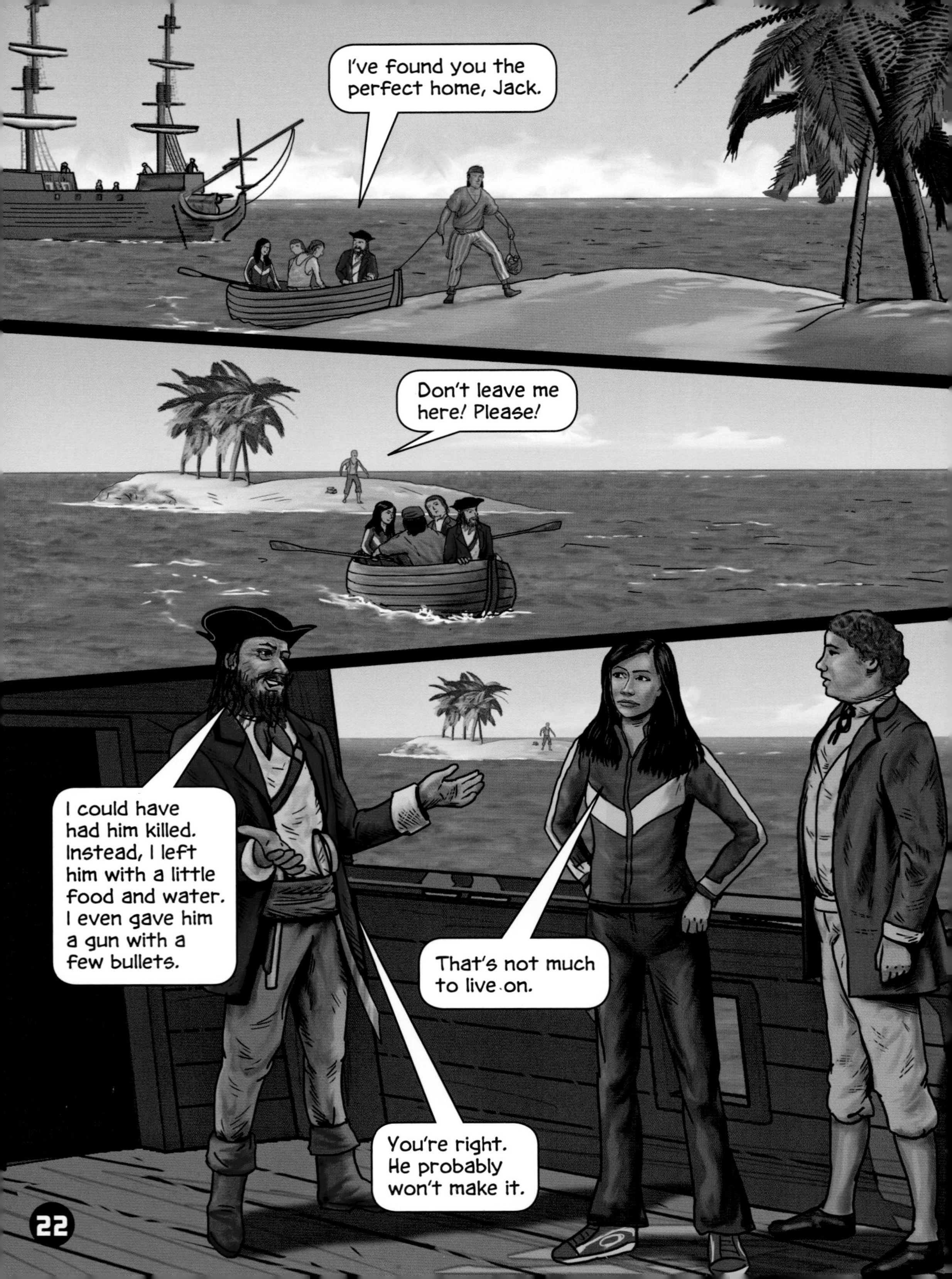
I've found you the perfect home, Jack.
Don't leave me here! Please!
I could have had him killed. Instead, I left him with a little food and water. I even gave him a gun with a few bullets.
That's not much to live on.
You're right. He probably won't make it.

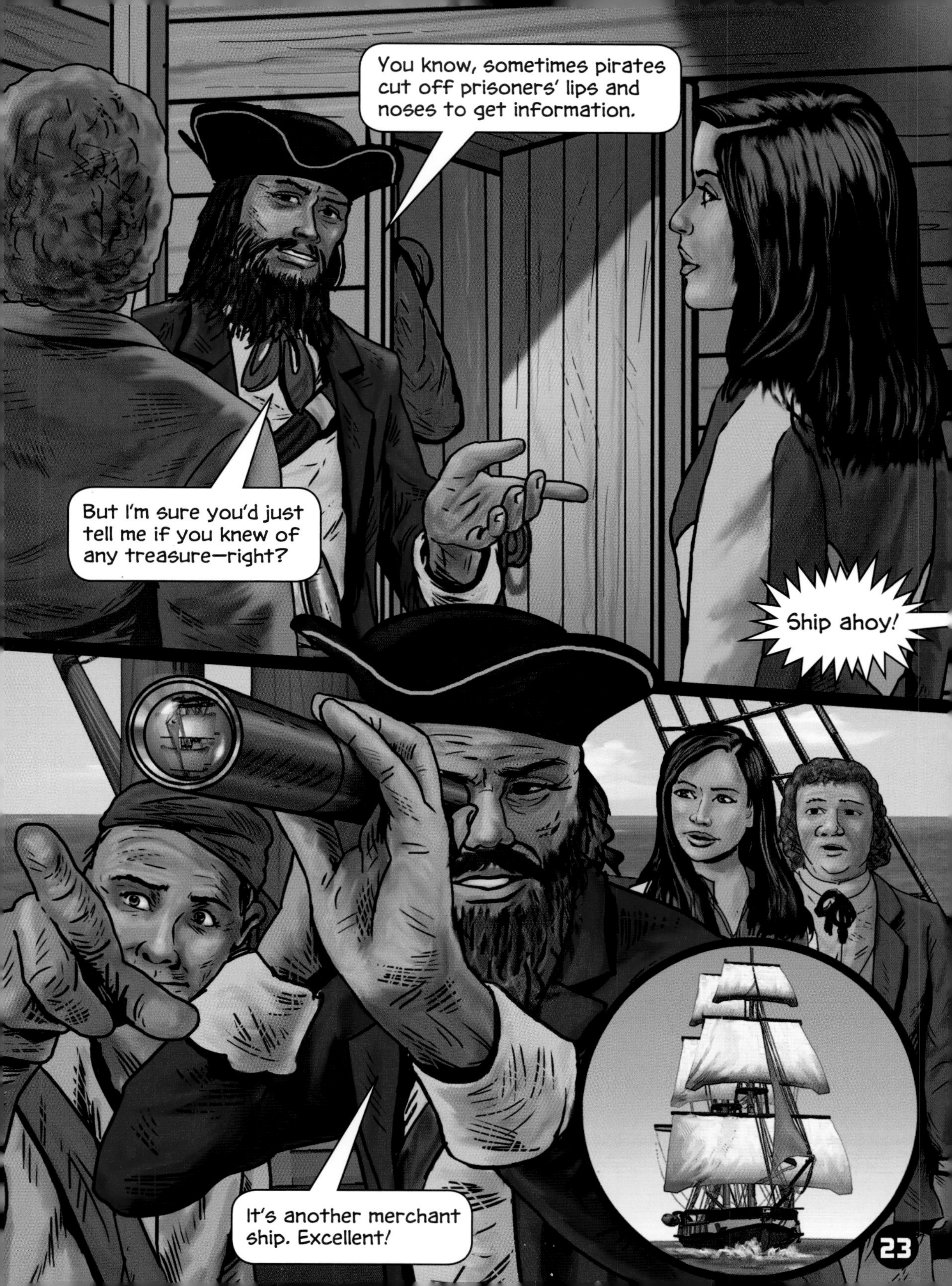
You know, sometimes pirates cut off prisoners' lips and noses to get information.
But I'm sure you'd just tell me if you knew of any treasure—right?
Ship ahoy!
It's another merchant ship. Excellent!

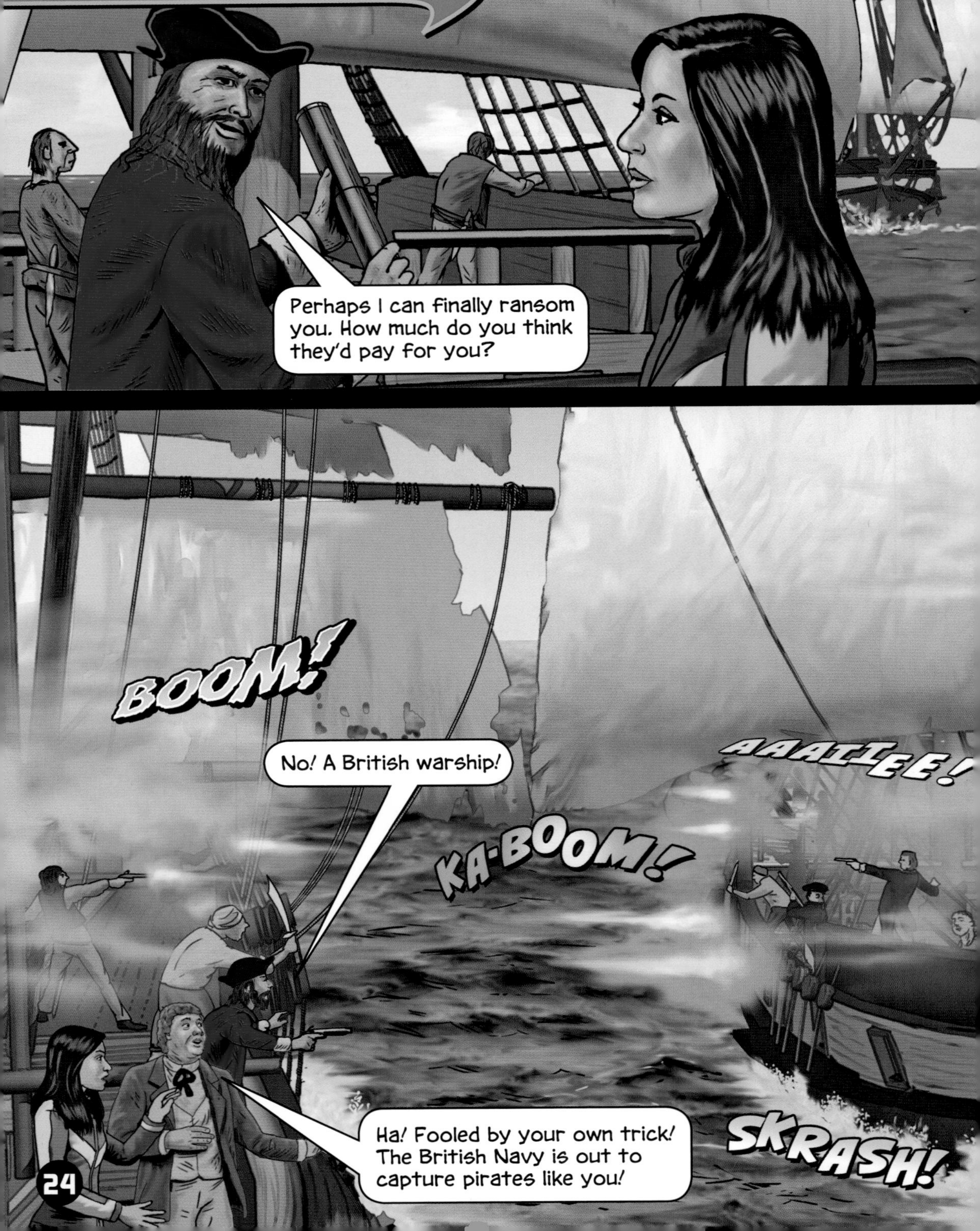
Perhaps I can finally ransom you. How much do you think they'd pay for you?
BOOM!
No! A British warship!
AAAIIEEE!
KA-BOOM!
Ha! Fooled by your own trick! The British Navy is out to capture pirates like you!
SKRASH!

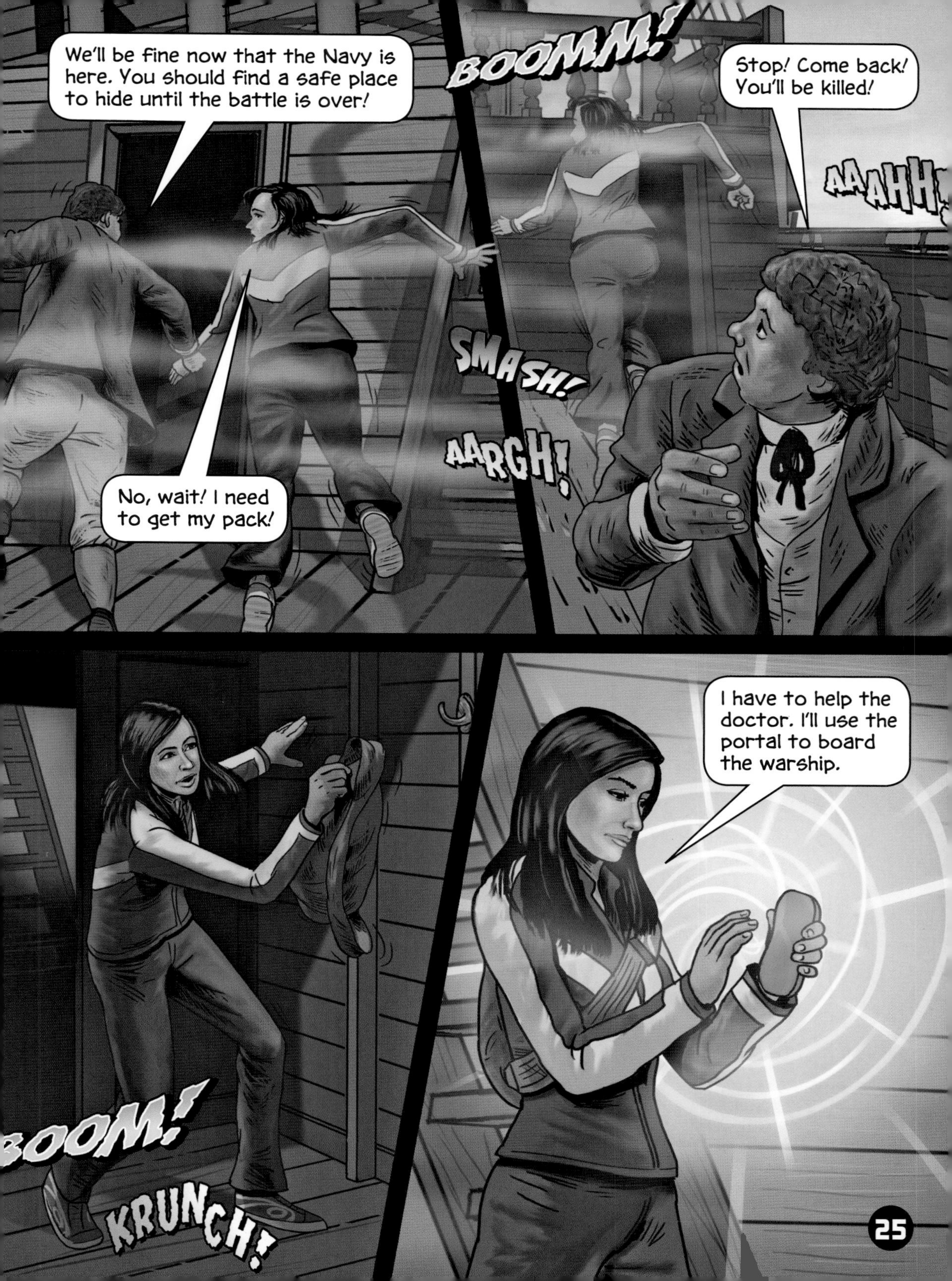
We'll be fine now that the Navy is here. You should find a safe place to hide until the battle is over!
No, wait! I need to get my pack!
BOOMM!
Stop! Come back! You'll be killed!
SMASH!
AARGH!
BOOM!
KRUNCH!
I have to help the doctor. I'll use the portal to board the warship.

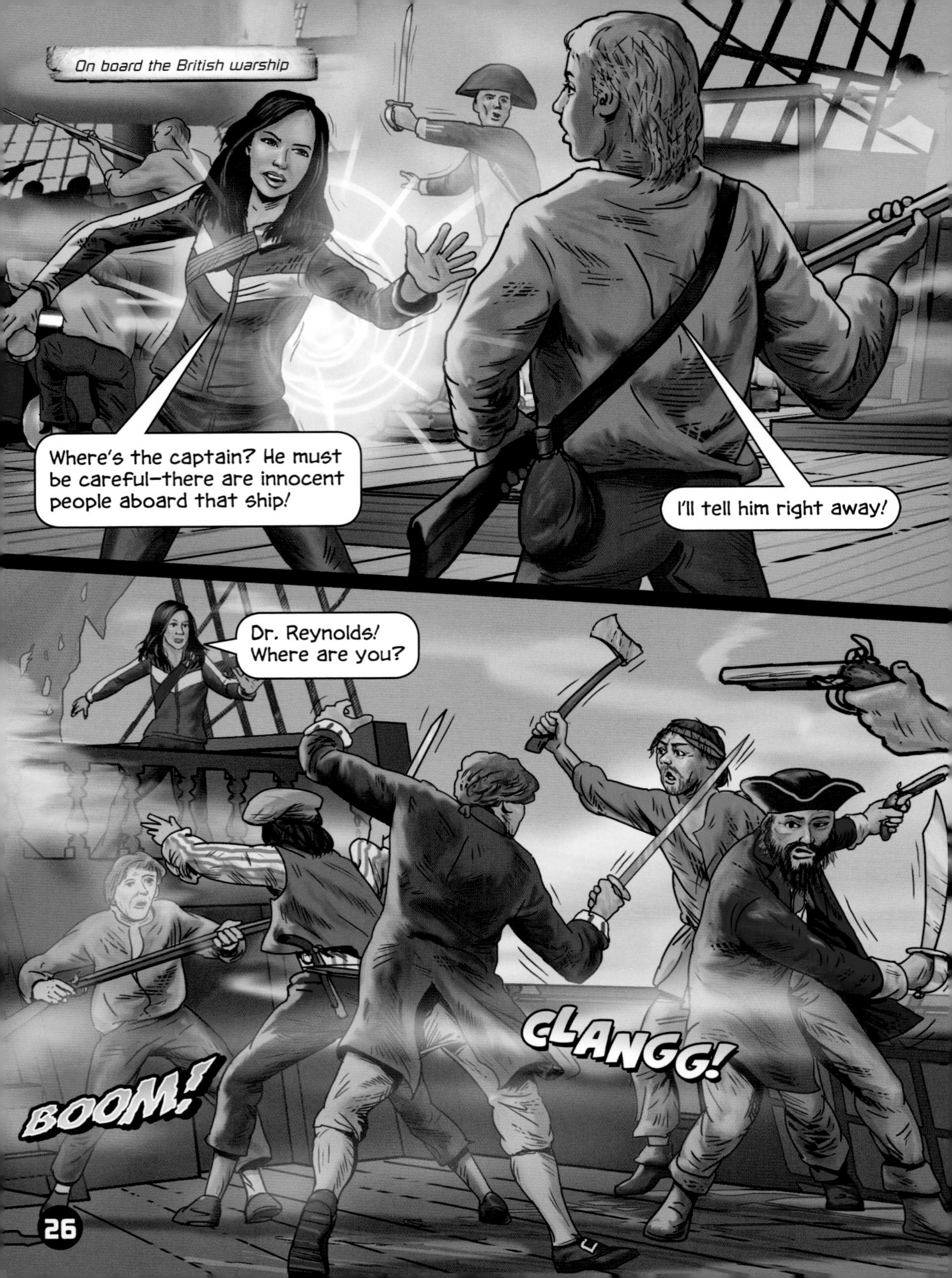
On board the British warship
Where's the captain? He must be careful—there are innocent people aboard that ship!
I'll tell him right away!
Dr. Reynolds! Where are you?
CLANGG!
BOOM!

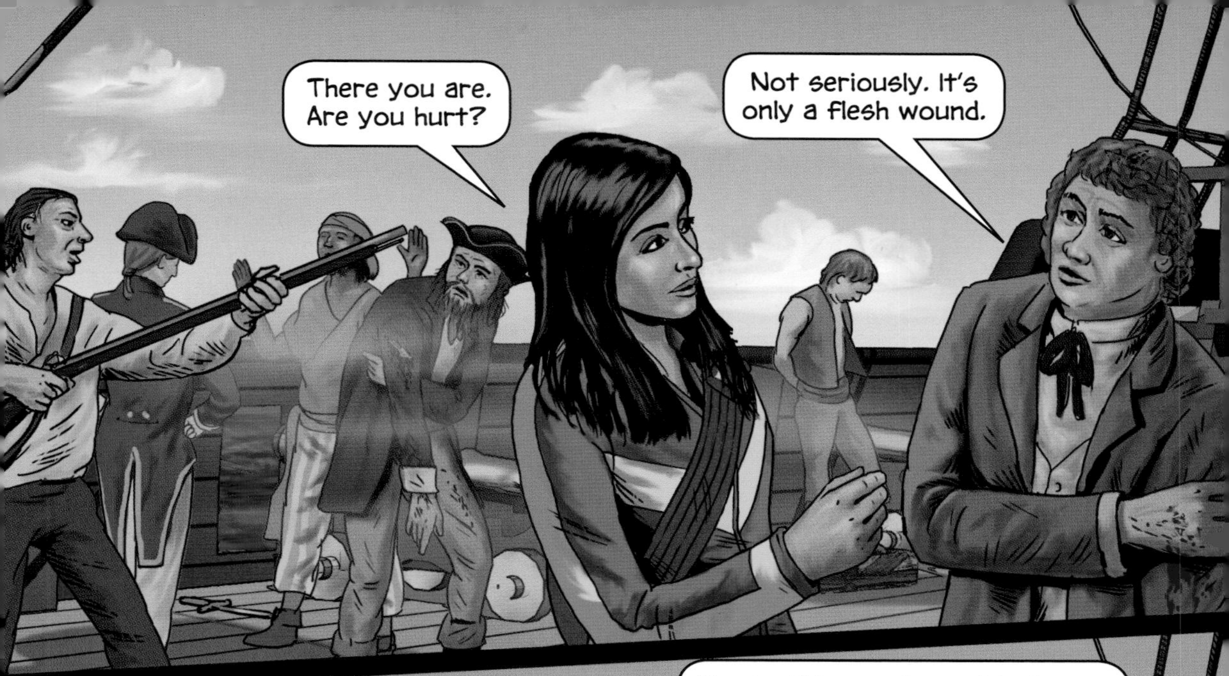
There you are. Are you hurt?
Not seriously. It's only a flesh wound.

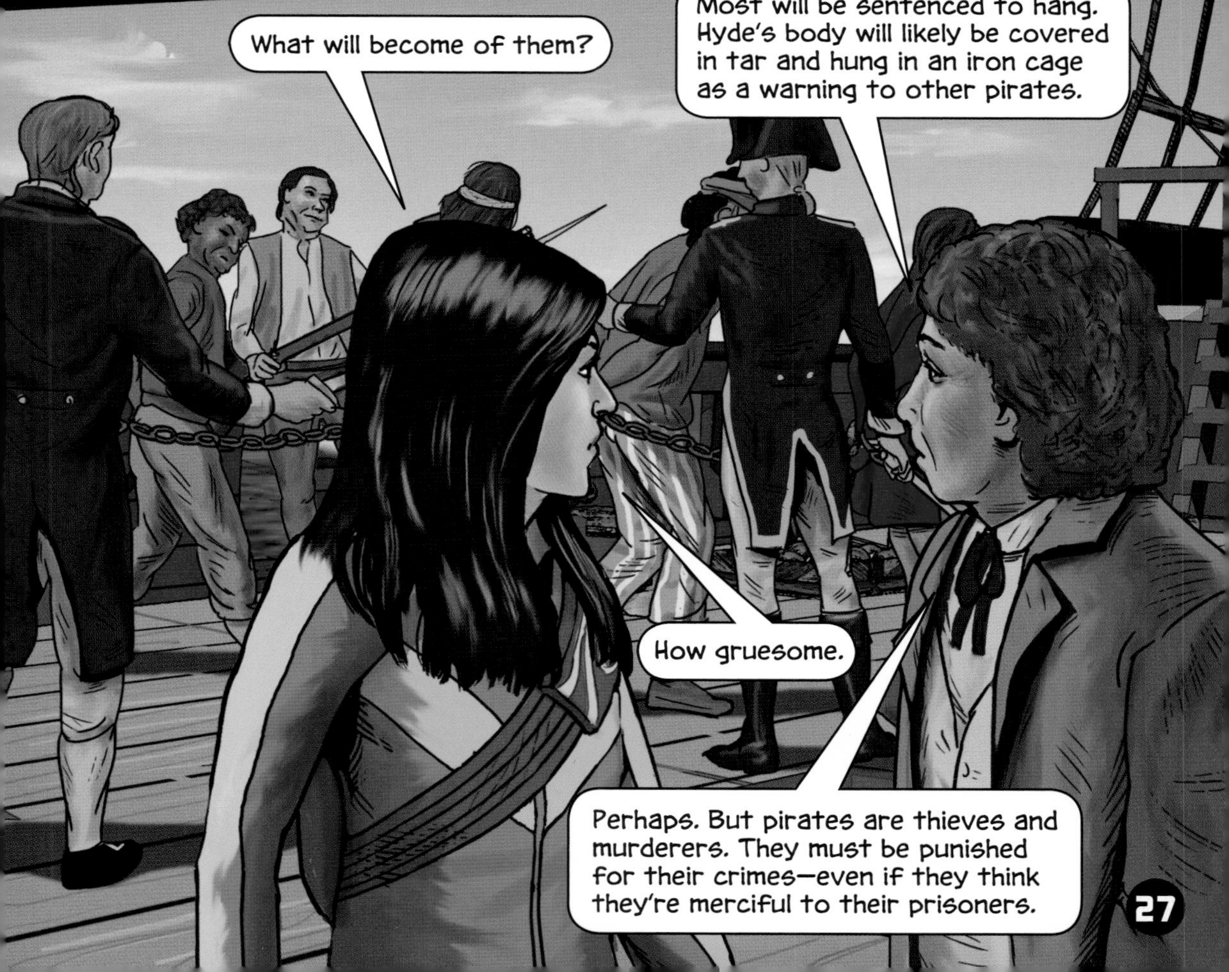
What will become of them?
Most will be sentenced to hang. Hyde's body will likely be covered in tar and hung in an iron cage as a warning to other pirates.
How gruesome.
Perhaps. But pirates are thieves and murderers. They must be punished for their crimes—even if they think they're merciful to their prisoners.

MORE ABOUT PIRATES

Until the 1800s, many governments issued letters of marque to private ships. These licenses allowed them to plunder enemy merchant ships. Such "legal pirates" were known as privateers. Privateers were only allowed to attack enemy vessels during wartime. But when wars ended, some privateers turned to piracy.

Sir Francis Drake was one famous privateer who worked for Queen Elizabeth I. Drake raided Spanish ships for treasure in the late 1500s. The British people considered him a hero. But to Spaniards, he was a cruel pirate.

Pirates voted democratically on all their activities. They even elected their captain and could remove him if they were unhappy with his leadership. To keep order aboard ship, pirates made up their own code of laws. The code explained the rules of the ship and how the pirates were to share their loot. It made clear how injured pirates were to be paid. The code also detailed the punishments for breaking any pirate laws.

There weren't many female pirates in history. Anne Bonny and Mary Read are among the few. During battles they wore men's clothing and fought alongside men. Bonny and Read were captured in 1720 with their captain, "Calico Jack" Rackham, and the rest of his crew. Bonny and Read's lives were spared because they were both pregnant. Read died in prison, but Bonny's fate remains unknown.

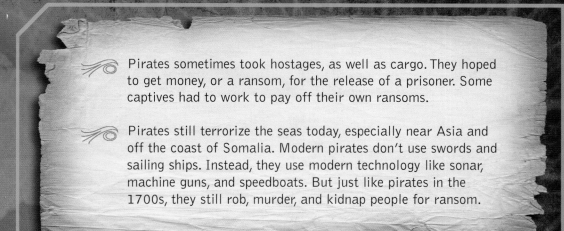

Pirates sometimes took hostages, as well as cargo. They hoped to get money, or a ransom, for the release of a prisoner. Some captives had to work to pay off their own ransoms.

Pirates still terrorize the seas today, especially near Asia and off the coast of Somalia. Modern pirates don't use swords and sailing ships. Instead, they use modern technology like sonar, machine guns, and speedboats. But just like pirates in the 1700s, they still rob, murder, and kidnap people for ransom.

MORE ABOUT

Isabel Soto

NAME: Dr. Isabel "Izzy" Soto
DEGREES: History and Anthropology
BUILD: Athletic   **HAIR:** Dark Brown
EYES: Brown   **HEIGHT:** 5' 7"

W.I.S.P.: The Worldwide Inter-dimensional Space/Time Portal developed by Max Axiom at Axiom Laboratory.

BACKSTORY: Dr. Isabel "Izzy" Soto caught the history bug as a little girl. Every night, her grandfather told her about his adventures exploring ancient ruins in South America. He believed lost cultures teach people a great deal about history.

Izzy's love of cultures followed her to college. She studied history and anthropology. On a research trip to Thailand, she discovered an ancient stone with mysterious energy. Izzy took the stone to Super Scientist Max Axiom who determined that the stone's energy cuts across space and time. Harnessing the power of the stone, he built a device called the W.I.S.P. It opens windows to any place and any time. Izzy now travels through time to see history unfold before her eyes. Although she must not change history, she can observe and investigate historical events.

GLOSSARY

cat-o'-nine-tails (kat-uh-NAHYN-teylz)—a whip with nine knotted cords attached to a handle that was used for punishment

colony (KAH-luh-nee)—an area that has been settled by people from another country and is controlled by that country

hardtack (HARD-tak)—a hard, saltless biscuit once used as food rations for armies and on board ships

infection (in-FEK-shuhn)—an illness or disease caused by germs

keelhaul (KEEL-hawl)—to attach a rope to someone and pull him or her under the bottom of a ship as a punishment

kidnap (KID-nap)—to capture a person and keep him or her as a prisoner, usually until demands are met

letter of marque (LET-ur UHV MARK)—a legal document allowing a ship's captain to claim the cargoes of enemy ships

maroon (muh-ROON)—to leave someone alone on a deserted island; pirates marooned people as a punishment for breaking the rules

raid (RAYD)—to make a sudden, surprise attack

ransom (RAN-suhm)—money that is demanded before a captive person will be set free

sonar (SOH-nar)—a device that uses sound waves to find underwater objects; sonar stands for sound navigation and ranging

swab (SWAHB)—to clean the surface of something, such as the deck of a ship

weevil (WEE-vuhl)—a type of beetle that is destructive to nuts, fruits, grains, and plants

READ MORE

Matthews, John. *Pirates Most Wanted: Thirteen of the Most Bloodthirsty Pirates Ever to Sail the High Seas.* New York: Atheneum Books for Young Readers, 2007.

Platt, Richard. *Pirate.* Eyewitness Books. New York: DK Pub., 2007.

Price, Sean. *Pirates: Truth and Rumors.* Truth and Rumors. Mankato, Minn.: Capstone Press, 2011.

Steer, Dugald. *The Pirateology Handbook: A Course in Pirate Hunting.* Cambridge, Mass.: Candlewick Press, 2008.

Temple, Bob. *The Golden Age of Pirates: An Interactive History Adventure.* You Choose Books. Mankato, Minn.: Capstone Press, 2008.

INTERNET SITES

FactHound offers a safe, fun way to find Internet sites related to this book. All sites on FactHound have been researched by our staff.

Here's all you do:

Visit *www.facthound.com*

Type in this code: 9781429675451

Check out projects, games and lots more at
www.capstonekids.com

INDEX

battles, 5, 7, 8, 12, 18,
    24–27, 28
becoming a pirate, 16
Bonny, Anne, 28
British Navy, 24–27

captains, 4, 5, 8, 11, 12,
    14, 17, 18, 26, 28
cargo, 4, 11
carpenters, 18, 19
cooks, 19

daily life, 4, 15–17
    dangers at sea, 15
    life expectancy, 15
doctors, 4, 8, 18, 19, 20,
    21, 25, 26
Drake, Sir Francis, 28

female pirates, 28
food, 10, 11, 21, 22
freedom, 16, 20, 28

injuries, 9, 18–19, 27, 28

letters of marque, 28
loot. *See* treasure

merchant ships, 4, 23
modern pirates, 29

pirate code, 12, 16, 19, 28
pirate flags, 7
pirate ships, 6, 29
    sails, 11
prisoners
    ransoming of, 9, 17, 20,
        24, 29
    treatment of, 14–15, 17,
        23, 27, 29
privateers, 28
punishments, 7, 12–13, 15,
        17, 20, 23, 27, 28
    marooning, 13, 21–22

Rackham, "Calico Jack," 28
Read, Mary, 28

treasure, 6, 7, 9, 16, 17, 19,
    20, 23, 28